I'LL SHARE

By JENNA LAFFIN

Illustrated by TINA KUGLER

CANTATA
LEARNING

MANKATO, MINNESOTA

WWW.CANTATALEARNING.COM

CANTATA
LEARNING
MANKATO, MINNESOTA

Published by Cantata Learning
1710 Roe Crest Drive
North Mankato, MN 56003
www.cantatalearning.com

Library of Congress Control Number: 2014956898
978-1-63290-259-7 (hardcover/CD)
978-1-63290-411-9 (paperback/CD)
978-1-63290-453-9 (paperback)

I'll Share by Jenna Laffin
Illustrated by Tina Kugler

Book design, Tim Palin Creative
Editorial direction, Flat Sole Studio
Executive musical production and direction, Elizabeth Draper
Music arranged and produced by Musical Youth Productions

Printed in the United States of America.

VISIT

WWW.CANTATALEARNING.COM/ACCESS-OUR-MUSIC

TO SING ALONG TO THE SONG

Sharing is a part of having good **manners**. Sharing shows you care about what other people need or want. It also makes getting along with others easier.

Now turn the page, and sing along.

When I go to school,
and I bring snacks,
I'll share my cookies,
if my friend asks.

If I have some,

and someone else has none,

I'll share with them,

so we'll both have fun!

When I'm playing at home
with my games and toys,
I'll share with my sister
the ones that she **enjoys**.

If I have some,

and someone else has none,

I'll share with them,

so we'll both have fun!

When I go to the park,

and I bring a ball,

I'll ask my friends to play.

Sharing is fun for all!

15

If I have some,

and someone else has none,

I'll share with them,

so we'll both have fun!

When I play outside
after a big **snowstorm**,
I'll share my scarf with my friend,
so we both stay warm.

If I have some,

and someone else has none,

I'll share with them,

so we'll both have fun!

SONG LYRICS
I'll Share

When I go to school,
and I bring snacks,
I'll share my cookies,
if my friend asks.

If I have some,
and someone else has none,
I'll share with them,
so we'll both have fun!

When I'm playing at home
with my games and toys,
I'll share with my sister
the ones that she enjoys.

If I have some,
and someone else has none,
I'll share with them,
so we'll both have fun!

When I go to the park
and I bring a ball,
I'll ask my friends to play.
Sharing is fun for all!

If I have some,
and someone else has none,
I'll share with them,
so we'll both have fun!

When I play outside
after a big snowstorm,
I'll share my scarf with my friend,
so we both stay warm.

If I have some,
and someone else has none,
I'll share with them,
so we'll both have fun!

Pop
Musical Youth Productions

I'll Share

Verse

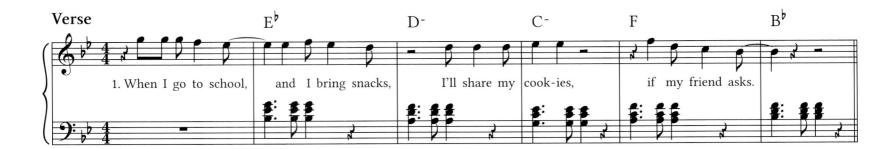

1. When I go to school, and I bring snacks, I'll share my cook-ies, if my friend asks.

Chorus

If I have some, and some-one else has none, I'll share with them, so we'll both have fun!

Verse 2
When I'm playing at home
with my games and toys,
I'll share with my sister
the ones that she enjoys.

Chorus

Verse 3
When I go to the park,
and I bring a ball,
I'll ask my friends to play.
Sharing is fun for all!

Chorus

Verse 4
When I play outside
after a big snowstorm,
I'll share my scarf with my friend,
so we both stay warm.

Chorus

GLOSSARY

enjoys—really likes doing something

manners—the way a person behaves around other people

sharing—letting someone use something or giving them part of what you have

snowstorm—a storm with a lot of wind and snow

GUIDED READING ACTIVITIES

1. Who is the illustrator of this book? What is your favorite illustration, and why?

2. List some of the things that are shared in this story.

3. Do you share with your friends and family? What do you share with them? What do they share with you?

TO LEARN MORE

Deen, Marilyn. *Share and Be Fair.* North Mankato, MN: Capstone Press, 2012.

Garland, Sally Anne. *Share.* Berkeley, CA: Owlkids Books, 2015.

Gassman, Julie. *Eleanore Won't Share.* Mankato, MN: Picture Window Books, 2011.

Lester, Helen. *All for Me and None for All.* Boston: Houghton Mifflin Harcourt, 2012.